ABOUT THE BOOK

Welcome to the colorful world of vegetables! 🥕🍅🥦 This book is an engaging educational tool filled with animated pictures and interactive illustrations to help children learn and identify various vegetables. Whether at home, in the classroom, or during playtime, it fosters a love for healthy eating and encourages active engagement in learning.

CARROT

CABBAGE

CABBAGE
BRINJAL

GREEN PEAS

TURNIP

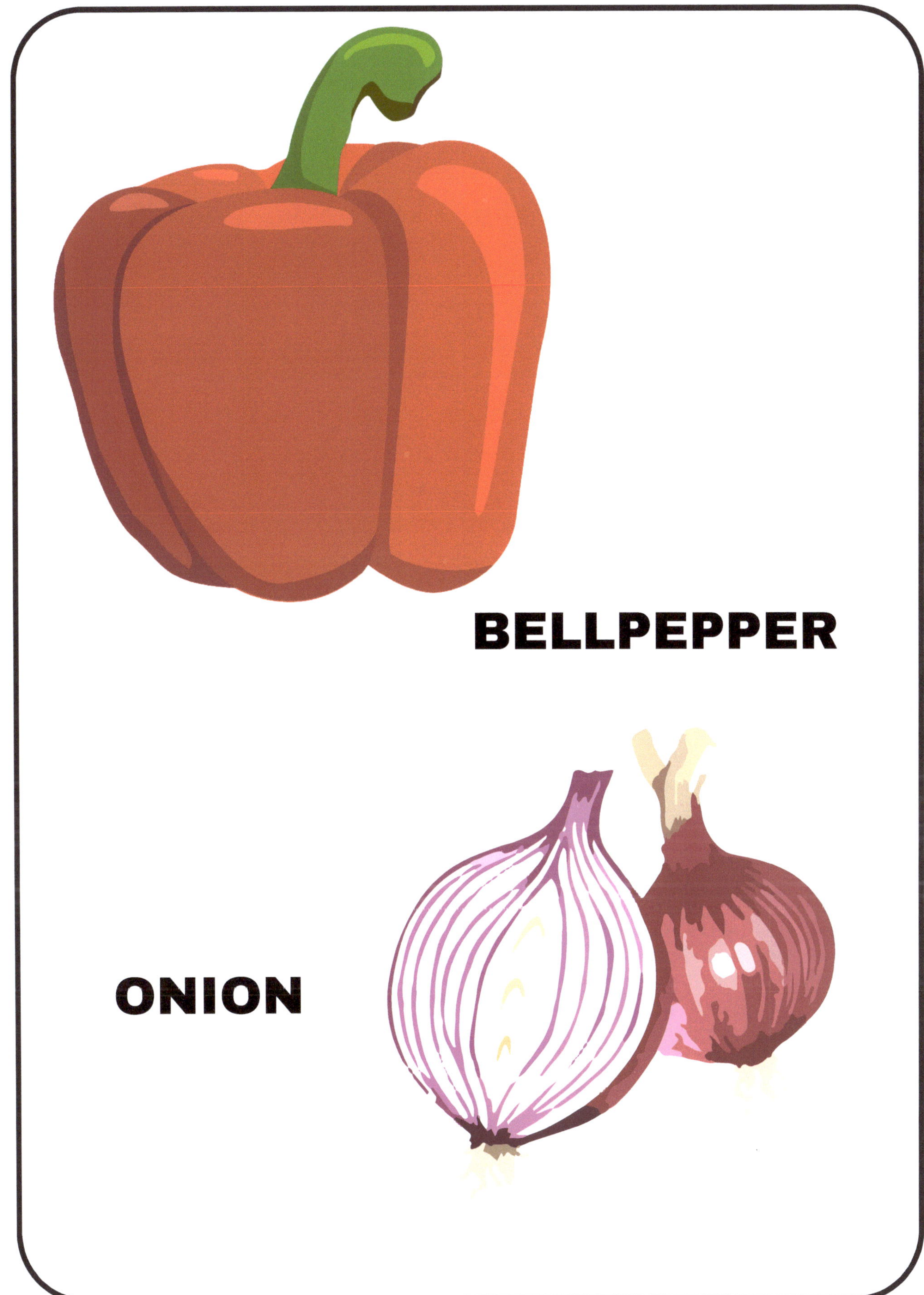
BELLPEPPER
ONION

GARLIC

RED CHILLIES

PUMPKIN

ZUCHINI
POTATO
CAULI FLOWER

LETTUCE

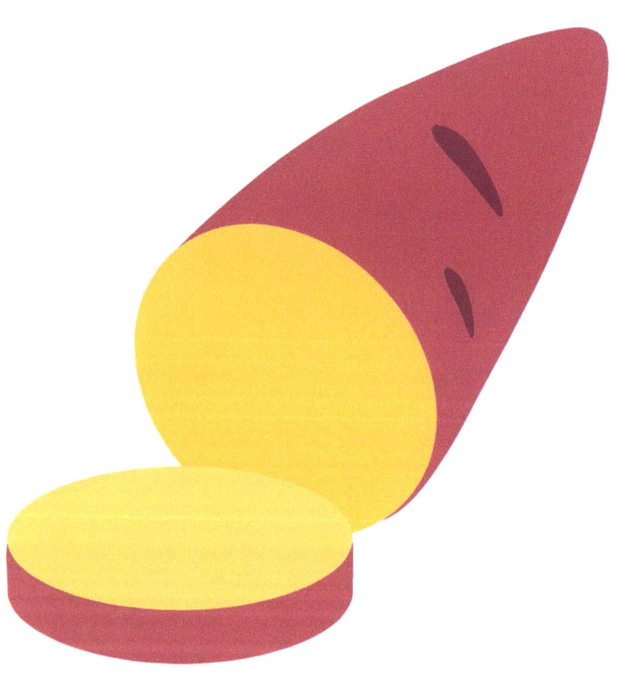

SWEET POTATO

BELL PEPPERS

CUCUMBER

Tell Tell, Who am I?

Tell Tell, Who am I?

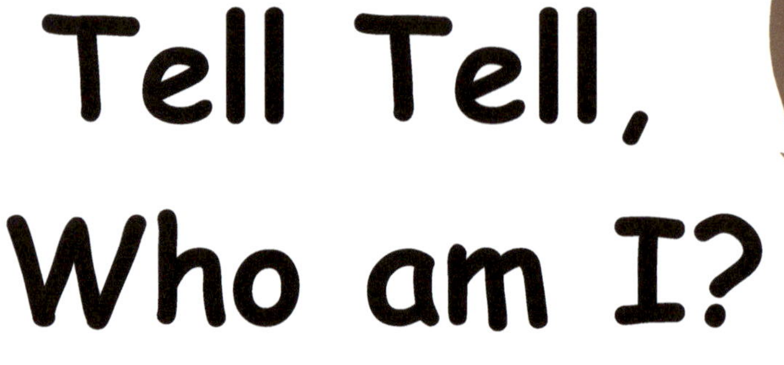
Tell Tell,
Who am I?

Tell Tell, Who am I?

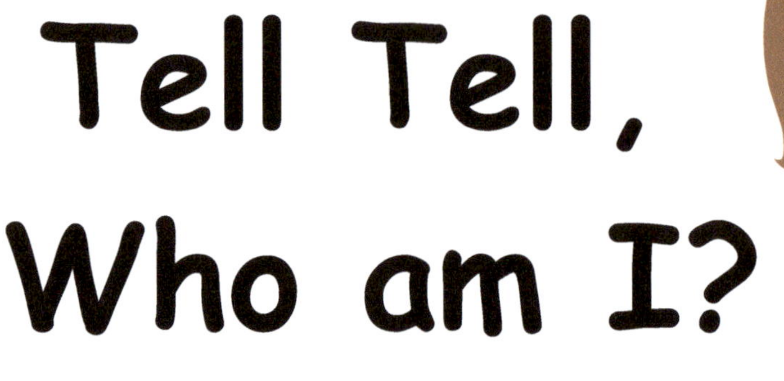
Tell Tell,
Who am I?

Tell Tell, Who am I?

Tell Tell, Who am I?

Tell Tell, Who am I?

Tell Tell, Who am I?

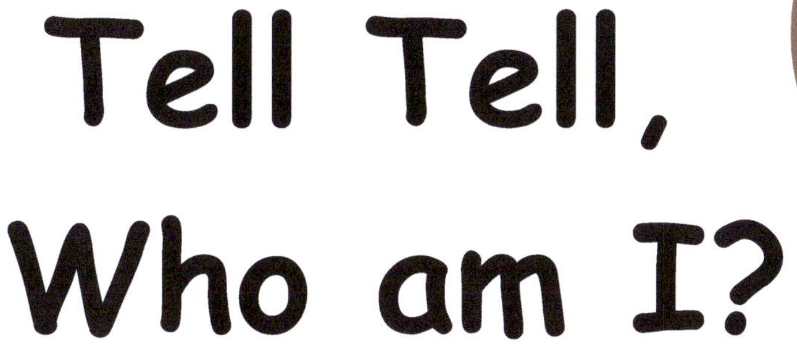
Tell Tell,
Who am I?

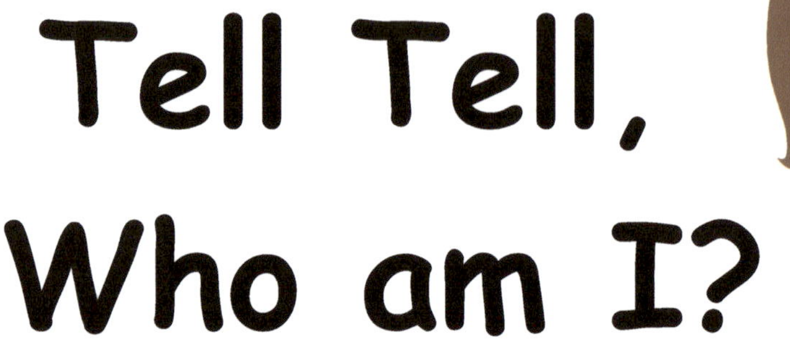
Tell Tell,
Who am I?

Tell Tell, Who am I?

Tell Tell, Who am I?

Tell Tell, Who am I?

Tell Tell,
Who am I?

Tell Tell,
Who am I?

Tell Tell,
Who am I?

Tell Tell, Who am I?

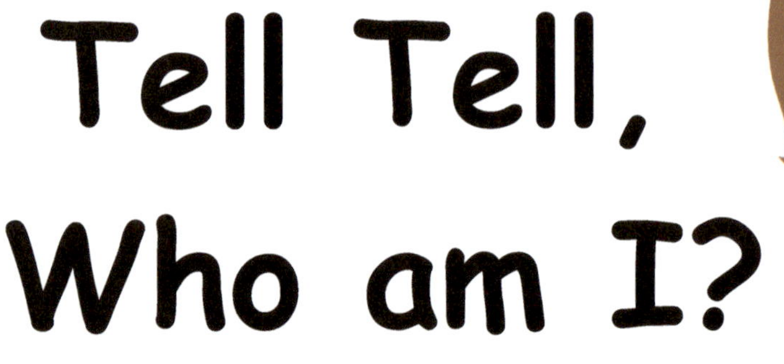
Tell Tell,
Who am I?

ABOUT THE AUTHOR

Nisha is an educational professional with a fervor for storytelling and a background in science. She loves storytelling in her classrooms and loves to work on the social-emotional learning of young minds. She loves to create helpful content for learning and reading. She believes in making this world a better place by sensitizing people with better teaching-learning-knowing processes. should you have any suggestions, write us at nishawrites18@gmail.com. Your feedback and suggestions are important to us. Happy reading.

www.ingramcontent.com/pod-product-compliance
Lightning Source LLC
LaVergne TN
LVHW071234160826
845679LV00003B/986

* 9 7 9 8 8 8 2 1 2 2 0 5 7 *